THE WORLD OF SCIENCE
INSECTS
AND THEIR RELATIVES

THE WORLD OF SCIENCE
INSECTS
AND THEIR RELATIVES

MAURICE BURTON

Facts On File Publications
New York, New York ● Bicester, England

INSECTS AND THEIR RELATIVES

First published in the United States of America in
1984 by Facts on File, Inc., 460 Park Avenue South,
New York, N.Y.10016

First published in Great Britain in 1984 by Orbis
Publishing Limited, London

**Library of Congress Cataloging in Publication
Data**

Main entry under title:

The world of science.

Includes index.
Summary: A twenty-five volume encyclopedia of
scientific subjects, designed for eight- to twelve-year-
olds. One volume is entirely devoted to projects.
1. Science—Dictionaries, Juvenile.   1. Science—
Dictionaries
Q121.J86   1984   500   84-1654

ISBN: 0-87196-986-6

Printed in Yugoslavia
10 9 8 7 6 5 4 3

Previous pages Close-
up of the giant stag
beetle

Consultant editors
Eleanor Felder, former managing editor, *New Book of
Knowledge*
James Neujahr, Dean of the School of Education, City
College of New York
Ethan Signer, Professor of Biology, Massachusetts
Institute of Technolgy
J. Tuzo Wilson, Director General, Ontario Science
Centre

Editor Penny Clarke
Designer Roger Kohn

CONTENTS

▼Two social wasps at work building their nest

1 WHAT ARE INSECTS?

2 DIFFERENT KINDS OF INSECT

3 INSECT RELATIVES

Note There are some unusual words in this book. They are explained in the Glossary on page 62. The first time each word is used in the text it is printed in *italics*.

WHAT ARE INSECTS?

INSECTS ARE ...

There are well over a million different kinds of insect in the world. We see them everywhere, on land, in the ground, in the air. Yet only one kind of insect lives on the sea, 'skipping' about on the surface hundreds of miles from land. On land they live on trees and other plants, in soil, in rivers and lakes, in deep underground caves, in hot springs, in scorching deserts and on ice-cold glaciers. And one insect, the petroleum fly, even lives in petroleum springs, eating other insects that have fallen into the springs.

Animals without backbones
Insects are *invertebrates*. That is, they are animals without backbones, but they have a tough outer skin or cuticle, rather like horn or fingernails. The cuticle acts as a kind of external skeleton to support the organs and muscles. It is waterproof and prevents the insect's body from drying up.

The word 'insect' is from Latin and means 'cut into'. The body of an insect seems cut into three parts: the head,

thorax and *abdomen*. Another thing to look for is the number of legs. Fully grown insects have three pairs of legs. Spiders, millipedes and woodlice look like insects but they have more than six legs. People often call spiders insects but they have four pairs of legs.

The head carries a mouth and mouth-parts. The mouth-parts may be jaws for chewing, a tongue for licking or a tube for sucking. On the sides of the head are usually a pair of large compound eyes, that is, eyes made up of many parts, known as facets. Some insects have also a few simple eyes on top of the head. The *antennae*, or feelers, are important sense organs. These are made up of many joints and are used for smell and touch, for finding food or a mate.

A few insects, like grasshoppers, have ears but these are usually on the legs or sides of the body.

The thorax bears the three pairs of legs and, on most insects, it has one or two pairs of wings. The wings are thin membranes, stiffened by networks of

►Diagram of an ant showing the three parts into which an insect's body is divided.

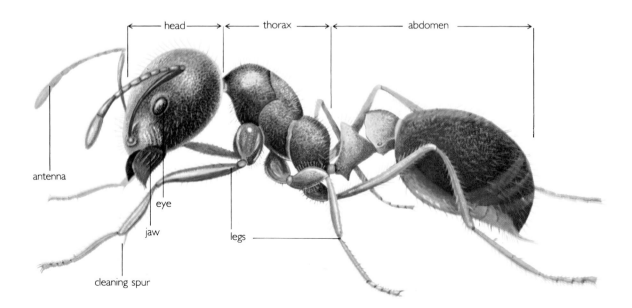

6

◄Close-up of the head of a horsefly. The two large green domes are compound eyes, each made up of many different units. Although they are large for the size of the insect's body, horseflies do not see very well.

▼The great diving beetle belongs to a family of insects that lives entirely in water and preys on other water creatures, sometimes much larger than itself. The hind legs have fringes of hairs and are used for swimming. The larvae are also aquatic and have large sickle-shaped jaws, which they use to capture their prey – insects, tadpoles or small fish.

veins and operated by muscles in the thorax. There are only two other kinds of animal that fly. These are birds and bats. Flying fishes and flying squirrels only glide. They do not beat their wings as insects do.

The abdomen is the largest section of the body. It contains the digestive, reproductive and excretory organs. Insects have no lungs. Instead on the sides of the abdomen are rounded holes. Air is drawn in through these holes and is carried all through the body by branching tubes.

7

FEEDING AND DIGESTION

There are so many different kinds of insect it is not surprising that they eat a wide variety of foods. Indeed, there is hardly any plant or animal that is not eaten by one insect or another. Many insects eat only living plants, others feed on living animals and large numbers live on dead plants or animals or on animal excrement. Some, such as cockroaches, will take almost anything, plant or animal, dead or alive, but most insects keep to one particular kind of food. For example, the caterpillars of the cabbage white butterfly eat only plants of the cabbage family. But no matter what they eat, insects, particularly when they are

larvae, are like other animals and need carbohydrates and fats to give them energy, proteins for growth, as well as vitamins and *trace elements*.

Different ways of feeding

The way an insect feeds depends entirely on what it eats. Some insects chew solid food and some suck liquid food. Each kind of insect deals with its food by means of special mouth-parts. For example, cockroaches, grasshoppers and beetles have two pairs of jaws. These, unlike our own jaws, are outside the mouth. The first pair are called the *mandibles*. They are large and strong for biting off pieces of food. The second pair are called *maxillae* and are used for chewing the food up small and passing it back to the mouth. In front of the mandibles is a lip, called the *labrum*, and behind the maxillae is a second lip, called the *labium*. The lips are used for tasting and guiding food into the mouth. Two pairs of finger-like *palps* help the lips guide the food.

The aphid is a very common insect in the garden, and elsewhere. The best known kinds are called greenfly and blackfly. They feed by sucking the sap from the leaves and tender stems. Their mouth-parts look like a tube and the sap

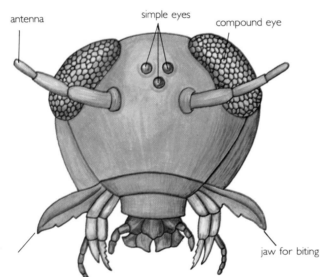

▶Insects that feed on plants, such as grasshoppers, have saw-edged jaws for nibbling. They also have several pairs of other mouth-parts for holding the pieces and passing them into the mouth.

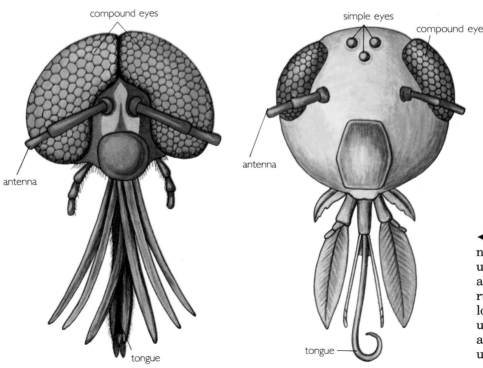

▶Insects that suck blood or liquids such as sap have piercing and sucking mouth-parts. The piercing mouth-parts are like very fine needles. The rest of the mouth-parts form a tube for sucking up the liquids.

◀Butterflies feed on nectar which they suck up from flowers using a tubular tongue. As a rule this tongue is very long and when not in use is carried coiled in a spiral on the underside of the head.

is sucked as if through a straw. The tube is made up of mandibles, maxillae, lips and palps which lock together to form two tubes. One is used for injecting saliva into the food to dissolve it. The other is used for sucking up the dissolved food.

Butterflies and moths feed on *nectar*, the sweet fluid made by plants. They have long tongues made up of long maxillae to suck the nectar from flowers. When these insects are not feeding their tongues are coiled below the head. Other sucking insects are the mosquitoes and fleas, and those, like the tsetse flies, that suck blood from cattle in Africa. They have long sharp mandibles and maxillae that pierce the skin. They inject saliva into the blood and then suck it up, mainly with the tongue.

The digestive system
The digestive system of both *larva* and adult insect is a continuous tube divided into foregut, midgut and hindgut. The first and last of these is lined with a cuticle, like that covering the body. The foregut stores food, at the same time breaking it up into smaller particles. It also passes the food onto the midgut, where it is digested. The midgut has no cuticle lining. Instead, it is lined with a thin membrane through which liquids can pass. So food substances are absorbed through its wall into the blood which carries them to the rest of the body. Finally, the undigested remains of food are passed into the hindgut to be ejected through the anus.

Insect larvae eat enormous quantities of food, because they are growing fast. Once the larvae become adults, growth ceases. Adult insects need mainly energy foods. There are some adult insects who do not feed at all. They live off fat stored when they were still larvae. Other insects take food in the form of carbohydrates, especially sugary foods, such as nectar. The larvae of wasps, for example, are fed by the worker wasps on protein-rich bluebottle flies and insects. But when the larvae turn into adults they feed on the nectar of flowers. This is very sugary and gives them the energy to fly. This need for sweet things explains why wasps come to jampots and rotten fruit.

▲Photograph of the front part of a grasshopper feeding on a blade of grass. It is holding the grass with its front legs while the strong jaws chew it. The rest of the mouthparts are hidden behind the jaws.

HOW INSECTS BREATHE

Insects and people breathe in entirely different ways. Unlike people, insects do not have lungs, and they do not take in air through the nose or mouth.

In our bodies, the oxygen in our lungs is absorbed into the blood and carried round the body in blood vessels. The blood is pumped through blood vessels by the heart.

Insects do not have arteries and veins. Their blood just fills the inside of the body. The stomach, intestine and other organs are bathed in blood, although there is a heart which keeps the blood on the move. As it is, an insect's blood system is not very efficient, and so is not very good at transporting oxygen. This is one of the reasons why insects are small. Most are less than 6mm (¼in) long and the largest insects living today are not more than 10cm (4in) long.

An insect's breathing system is completely different from ours. Along each side of an insect's body is a line of tiny holes. They look like the portholes of a ship. These holes are called *spiracles*, and they lead into tubes. Each tube has several branches and the branches run to all parts of the body. Air containing oxygen enters the spiracles and is carried to the organs and muscles through the network of tubes.

Very active insects have a way of increasing the flow of air in the tubes. They need plenty of oxygen for flying. Some of the tubes are expanded to form air sacs like small balloons and the insect makes pumping movements so that the 'balloons' work like bellows to pump air along the tubes. If you are patient it is quite easy to see bees and wasps pumping their abdomens.

Breathing under water

Some insect larvae live in water. Mosquito and dragonfly larvae spend all their time in water, but have quite different ways of breathing. The mosquito larva has a tube at the hind end of the body. From time to time it swims up to the surface, pokes this tube into the air and takes in a supply of oxygen. The dragonfly larva has gills. These are flaps at the tail end of the body. The larva pumps water over these gills to take in oxygen.

Water beetles that spend all their lives in water come to the surface, push the tail end into the air and lift their wing cases. This means they dive again with a supply of air under their wing cases which may last several minutes. It is like the aqualung diver who takes his cylinders of oxygen down with him.

Other water insects trap a bubble of air which spreads thinly over the body and makes them look silvery. The bubble acts as a kind of gill. As the insect uses up oxygen in its breathing system more oxygen passes from the water into the bubble and so through the spiracles.

►Drawing of an insect from the side showing the head, thorax and abdomen and other parts that make up the body. Along the side of the abdomen are the openings, known as spiracles, through which it takes in air.

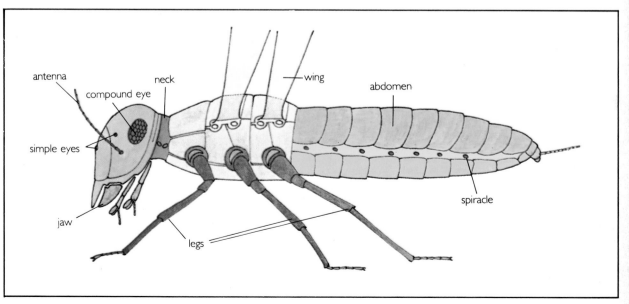

antenna
compound eye
neck
wing
abdomen
simple eyes
jaw
legs
spiracle

10

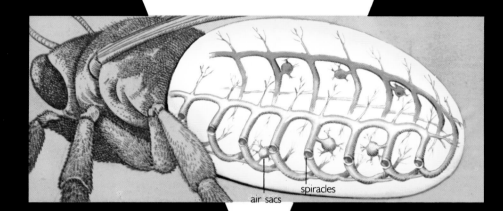

air sacs   spiracles

◄Drawing of the inside of an insect's body showing the branching tubes into which air passes as it enters through the spiracles (seen here as black dots on the nearest set of tubes).

►Grasshopper on a leaf, the line of breathing holes, or spiracles, can be seen along the side of its abdomen.

◄Insects or insect larvae that live in water either breathe by gills or come to the surface to take in air. These two mosquito larvae are each taking in air at the surface through a tube at their tail end.

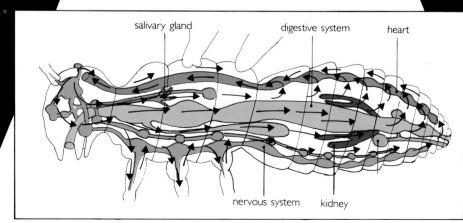

salivary gland   digestive system   heart

nervous system   kidney

◄The heart of an insect is a long tube running under the skin of its back from the head to the tail end. There are no other blood vessels. Blood leaves the heart to flow round the other organs.

THE SENSE ORGANS

We have eyes to see, ears to hear with, a nose for smelling and a tongue for tasting. Then there is the sense of touch which is in every part of our body. These are what we call our five senses.

We have a large brain and a system of nerves running throughout the body. The nerves carry messages from the sense organs to the brain to put us in touch with the world around us. They also tell us what is going on inside our body. Other nerves connect the brain with the muscles. Most nerves are linked to the brain by the spinal cord, the main nerve cord.

Insects have only a simple nerve system. There is a main nerve, running along the underside of the body, not in the back, like our spinal cord. The main nerve has a series of knots along its length. These are masses of nerve cells called *ganglia*. Each helps to control the part of the body around it. In the head there is a pair of slightly larger ganglia. These lie on top of the gut and are the nearest thing an insect has to a brain. They receive messages from the sense organs and help control the insect's behaviour. If an insect loses its head the rest of it will continue to live for a while.

Insects' eyes

The importance of the sense organs differs in various kinds of insect. Eyes are important for some, but others are blind and ants living underground can only see well enough to tell light from dark. Insects with poor eyesight, however, usually have a good sense of smell or are very sensitive to touch.

Insects' eyes vary, some have only tiny eyes, others have large ones. The tiny eyes are called simple eyes. The large ones are called compound eyes because they are compounded, or made up of, many small parts.

▶Antennae are the most important sense organs of insects. An insect smells with its antennae. It probably uses them also for touch. Different insects have different kinds of antennae – these are some examples.

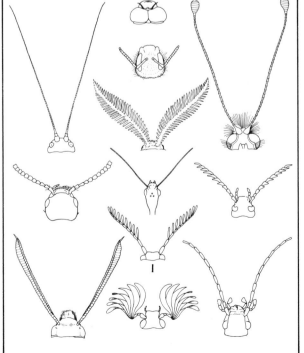

▲At the **top** is the head of a butterfly showing its clubbed antennae. In the picture **above** are the feathery antennae that larger moths have.

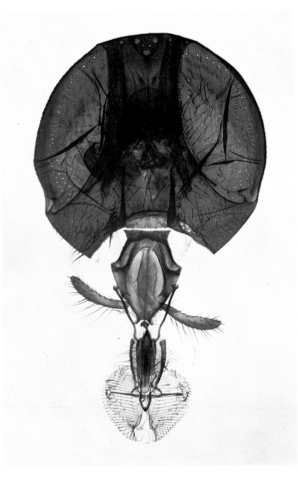

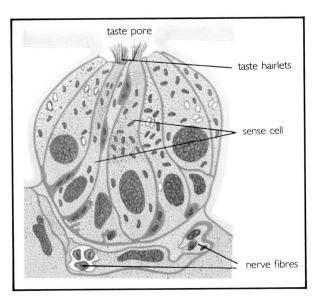

◄This photograph, taken under a microscope, shows the head of a bluebottle fly. Saliva is passed down the mouth-parts to mix with the food and digest it. It is then licked up with the elaborate tongue.

▶We are not sure how insects taste their food. We have taste buds on our tongue, one of which is shown here highly magnified. Insects have cells like these but they are even smaller. Some butterflies taste through their feet.

taste pore

taste hairlets

sense cell

nerve fibres

The large eyes of a dragonfly help it to see all round and a dragonfly can see an insect 10 metres (11 yards) away. Yet large as their eyes are, dragonflies cannot see as well as we can.

The one thing a compound eye is good for is detecting the slightest movement. Try catching a bluebottle on a window pane with your fingers!

Some insects can see colours well, but they may not see the same colours as we do. Honeybees, for example, cannot see reds or oranges, but they can see ultra-violet which is invisible to us.

Touch and taste

The sense of touch is present all over our body, but in insects it is concentrated into tiny hairs. If one of the hairs is bent, a message is sent along a nerve. A blue-bottle senses your hand is approaching because it sees the movement and the tiny breeze made by the moving hand bends the hairs on its body. The sense of taste is also contained in some of these hairs. A fly tastes what it is walking on

by means of hairs on its feet.

An insect has no nose, instead it smells with its antennae, or feelers. The feathery antennae of male moths are used to find the females. Only a minute amount of scent from the female makes the male fly in search of her.

Hearing

Feeling a slight breeze is a simple form of hearing, because sound consists of tiny movements of air. Mosquitoes detect the buzzing of the wings of other mosquitoes. The sound makes their antennae vibrate and send nerve messages to the brain. Each kind of mosquito buzzes at a slightly different pitch and male mosquitoes are sensitive only to the pitch of females of their own kind.

Grasshoppers, crickets and cicadas have special ears on the body or even the legs. Some moths also have good ears. They can hear the sonar squeaks of bats, which are too high-pitched for our ears. When a moth hears a bat coming it tries to escape because bats eat moths.

13

THE LIFE HISTORY OF INSECTS

▶Caterpillars of the emperor moth hatching from a batch of eggs laid on a leaf. Birds will eat most of them but a few will live to grow into adults.

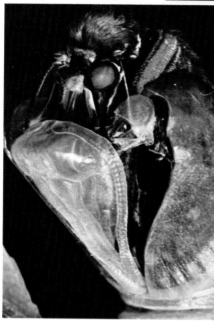

▲An adult butterfly forcing its way out of the pupa case. Note the lid that opens to let it out.

A new-born kitten looks very like its mother. You would never mistake it for a puppy, for example. A newly-hatched chick may not look exactly like the parent bird, but it is obvious that it is a bird. This is not so in the insect world.

From a very early age we can recognise a butterfly, but it may be a surprise to learn that a butterfly begins life as a caterpillar, a worm-like insect without wings. So, at some time in its life the caterpillar must undergo a complete change in shape. This is called a *metamorphosis*, which is the Greek word for transformation.

Most insects are divided into two groups. There are those, like butterflies, moths, beetles and flies which undergo a complete metamorphosis at some point in their life-history. The young stage, or larva, is very different from the adult. The others, and they include dragonflies, grasshoppers and *bugs*, have an incomplete metamorphosis. Instead, the young stages are not very different from the adult and the growing insect undergoes several small changes.

As soon as a female insect lays her eggs the larvae begin to develop inside. When each larva is fully formed the egg is ready to hatch. The larva swallows air or liquid and, by pulling in its abdomen, squeezes this into the front end of the body. As the front end swells it presses on the inside of the shell until it splits. Then the larva can crawl out. Some larvae have special egg bursters on their heads to help tear through the shell.

As soon as it is hatched the larva begins to feed and grow. Because it has a rigid cuticle its body cannot expand. So it moults. That is, the tough skin splits and the larva crawls out of it. A new cuticle has already grown under the old one and the larva's body swells to fill it. This casting of the old skin is called the moult.

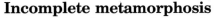

1 **2** **3** **4**

Incomplete metamorphosis

Insects that have an incomplete metamorphosis moult several times before the insect has reached full size. At the same time the wings are growing by easy stages. At first they are no more than tiny buds on the back of the thorax. They grow bigger at each moult until they have reached full size. The number of moults may be as few as four or as many as thirty, but the larva and adult insects are not very different.

Complete metamorphosis

In insects that undergo complete metamorphosis there is a much greater difference between larva and adult. The larva hatching from the egg has such small legs they are not easy to see. The body does not seem to be divided into three distinct parts. A head can be seen but behind this the thorax and abdomen run into one, divided into rings or segments.

Sometimes the larva can only wriggle, and it is usually white or pale yellow. Such larvae are called *grubs* or *maggots*. Beetle larvae are usually called grubs and bluebottle larvae maggots.

The larvae of butterflies and moths are called caterpillars, a name that means 'hairy cat', because so many of them are hairy. Some caterpillars are large so it is easy to see how they are made. They have three pairs of legs, as is usual in insects. These are like claws, not jointed, and are on the front part of the body. They also have several pairs of legs on the rear end of the body. These are not true legs and are called *prolegs*. They are fleshy stubs by which the caterpillar can cling to a stem or leaf. Some caterpillars loop along. They grasp a stem with the front legs then draw the body into a loop to grasp the stem with the prolegs.

When a caterpillar has reached full size it changes into a *chrysalis*. Its skin changes colour and it loses its legs and prolegs. It can no longer move from place to place, so it rests. Many caterpillars spin a cocoon around themselves as they change to the chrysalis.

Inside the chrysalis an even greater change takes place. The muscles break down into a mush of tissue and the whole of its insides are rebuilt. In the course of this rebuilding, or pupation, the adult's six jointed legs and two pairs of wings appear. Instead of a simple eye on each side of the head, a large compound eye appears and a pair of antennae grow out of the head.

When this resting stage comes to an end, the chrysalis splits and out comes the butterfly or the moth in all its glory. The wings are still crumpled, so it hangs from a stem to allow time for the wings to stretch and dry. After this, the adult insect, so unlike the caterpillar from which it came, is ready to fly.

The main task of an adult insect is to mate. After mating, the female lays her eggs and the cycle begins all over again.

▶The life cycle of the monarch butterfly.
1 The eggs have hatched into caterpillars which eat green leaves. **2** When the caterpillar has stored all the energy it needs, it attaches itself to a twig and changes into a pupa. **3** As a pupa, the insect is encased in a tough skin and all its energies are concentrated on becoming an adult. **4** When this change is complete the adult breaks out of the skin and hangs limply waiting for its wings to dry. When they are dry it will fly away.

► The tsetse fly looks like a blowfly. It lives in Africa and causes sleeping sickness in people. It also gives diseases to cattle.

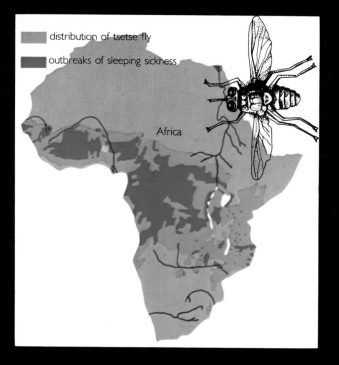

distribution of tsetse fly

outbreaks of sleeping sickness

Africa

▼ A swarm of locusts darkens the sky on the border between Kenya and Uganda. Some swarms in Africa have covered areas of up to 5,000 square kilometres (2,000 square miles) and eaten 20,000 tons of green plants in a single day!

distribution of tsetse fly

outbreaks of sleeping sickness

PESTS AND PLAGUES

There are insects that bite, insects that sting, insects that eat our crops, carry disease, attack farm animals and feed on our food when it is stored. It is hard to think of anything in our lives that may not, at some time or another, be hurt, damaged or destroyed by an insect.

Locusts – a terrifying plague

A locust is a large grasshopper that lives in swarms. Ordinary grasshoppers eat plants, but usually they do little damage. For most of the time locusts do little harm. But sometimes they breed very fast and huge swarms gather. There may be a thousand million in a swarm. As they fly they blot out the sun, darkening the sky. A swarm can fly as much as 50 kilometres (30 miles) a day.

In a few hours a swarm of locusts can strip large areas of grassland, eat every leaf off the trees or take a whole crop leaving only the soil. In the poorer areas of Africa and the Middle East, people have to struggle hard to grow enough food and a plague of locusts can bring famine. Today satellites are used to find locust swarms and aircraft to spray them with poison, so locust plagues are now rare.

Another pest is the Mediterranean fruit fly. It was accidentally carried from Europe to America where it became a pest in orchards.

Insects and disease

In the Middle Ages the Black Death swept across Europe. In some towns and villages nine people out of every ten died of the plague. Black rats carrying fleas had reached Europe from central Asia. The fleas carried the plague. People bitten by the fleas became ill and died. Their bodies went black, so giving the disease its nickname of 'Black Death'.

The plague is rare today, but insects cause other diseases. The tsetse flies of Africa carry a disease known as sleeping sickness. In a large part of Africa it is impossible to keep cattle because the tsetse fly bites them and gives them the disease. People can also get the disease.

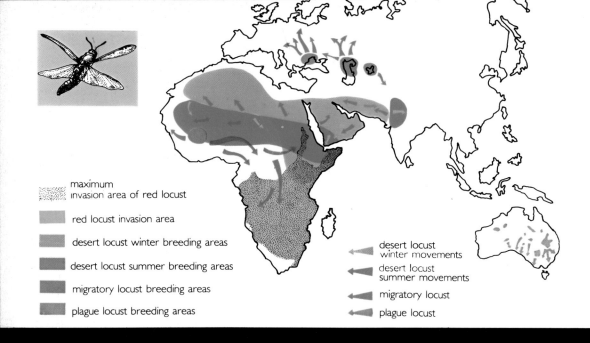

There are four main species of locust. This map shows their breeding areas and where they are likely to swarm.

maximum invasion area of red locust

red locust invasion area

desert locust winter breeding areas

desert locust summer breeding areas

migratory locust breeding areas

plague locust breeding areas

◀ **desert locust winter movements**

◀ **desert locust summer movements**

◀ **migratory locust**

◀ **plague locust**

The mosquito – a dangerous insect

A mosquito is only a tiny insect, but it is one of the world's most dangerous animals. It is a two-winged fly that annoys us by the way it buzzes round our head. Sometimes you can see mosquitoes 'dancing' in small swarms in the sunlight. This is their mating dance, when the males try to attract the females.

After mating the female lays her eggs, but before she can do this she must have a drink of blood. This is when she bites. Where she bites a little bump comes up on our skin and itches. It is not dangerous and soon disappears.

In warm countries mosquitoes often carry the germs of dangerous diseases, such as yellow fever and malaria. These diseases kill millions of people every year. To stop this great efforts are made to control the number of mosquitoes.

The female mosquito lays her eggs on water and the larvae live in the water. The water may be a lake, a marsh, a small puddle, or even the water in an old tin can. So, to fight against malaria and other diseases the first thing is to get rid of as much water as possible. Marshes where mosquitoes breed can be drained and the larvae in lakes and ponds killed by spraying insecticides on the water. But it is a hard battle, because every time it rains there is more water for the mosquitoes.

▼Stages in the metamorphosis of three medically important mosquitoes. The eggs look different and group together differently. The eggs hatch into larvae. The larvae of the *Anopheles* mosquito breathes through tiny holes in its body as it lies along the surface of the water. The larvae of *Culex* and *Aedes* have breathing tubes which they poke through the water's surface. The larvae become pupae and, finally, adults. *Culex* can transmit a disease called encephalitis, some kinds of *Aedes* transmit yellow fever, and some of the *Anopheles* mosquitoes are the ones that give us malaria.

anopheles

culex

aedes

2 DIFFERENT KINDS OF INSECT

USEFUL INSECTS

The world may seem full of dangerous insect pests, but there are many more that are useful and do good.

The importance of insects to flowers

The world can be a beautiful place, especially where there are trees and flowers. When the flowers die they leave behind their fruits, some of which are good to eat and important in our diet. But there would be no beautiful flowers and no sweet fruits without *pollen*. Pollen must be carried from one plant to another to pollinate, or fertilise, them so they will produce fruit. Some flowers are pollinated by the wind, but many have their pollen transported by insects, especially honeybees and bumble bees. If pollination is prevented, perhaps because cold weather kills the insects, fruit crops can fail.

▼A silk moth cocoon cut open to show the pupa.

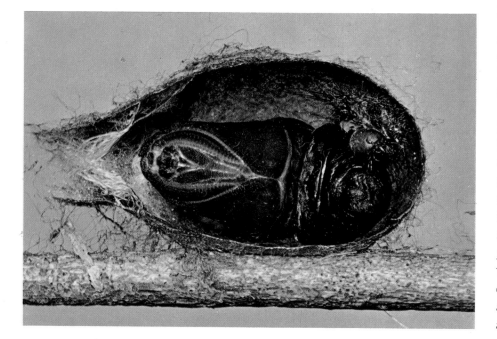

Cleaning up the countryside

Other insects help to keep the countryside clean and tidy. They are called scavengers. By feeding on dead plants and the bodies of dead animals they do two things. They get rid of dead material and in doing so break it up and return it to the soil, where it will feed new plants. Dung beetles and burying beetles (p 49) do this. A good example of the importance of beetles like the dung beetle happened in Australia. When people from Europe first went to live in Australia they took their cattle and sheep with them. There were no dung beetles then in Australia. As a result, the cattle dung just lay on the ground and took years to rot. So dung beetles were introduced into Australia to do the work.

Makers of silk

The dung beetle is not the first insect to be used by man. The silk worm, the caterpillar of the silk moth, has been used by the Chinese for five thousand years. The silk moth lays its eggs on the leaves of mulberry trees and the caterpillars feed on the leaves. When a caterpillar is fully grown it stops feeding and spins a cocoon of silk around itself. The cocoon is made up of a single strand of silk 900 m (about 1,000 yd) long. It can be unwound and used to spin silk cloth. By keeping the silk moth in special 'farms' and gathering the silk from the cocoons, this insect has become a domesticated animal. In the same way honeybees have been domesticated and used for making honey and beeswax.

Biological control

During the last hundred years another way has been found of making insects useful. This is by using one insect against another. In California the cottony cushion insect, or cottony scale, was introduced accidentally from Australia. It became a great pest. One of its enemies, a ladybird, was brought from Australia to try to control it. The experiment was a success and the cottony cushion is no longer such a serious pest.

▲A honeybee on the comb. The honeycomb is made of wax. When the honey has been drained from the comb the wax can be used in medicines; for making candles and for other useful things.

▶A ladybird laying her eggs. The larvae hatching from the eggs feed on aphids. So do the adult ladybirds. They are said to eat 14 times their own weight in a day.

▲A silk moth has just left the silken cocoon in which it pupated.

Even more striking was the way a plant pest was overcome using an insect. The prickly pear cactus was taken to Australia. Somebody had the idea it would be a cheap way of feeding cattle. The cactus did so well it started to spread. Within a few years it had covered millions of hectares and it seemed impossible to stop it.

A moth whose caterpillar eats prickly pear was taken to Australia. In two years several million hectares of the cactus were cleared by the caterpillars and the prickly pear is no longer a problem.

The use of animals or plants to control the growth and spread of pests and weeds is known as biological control. It is better than the use of chemicals for several reasons. One is that when the animal or plant, in this case the prickly pear, dies out so does the animal used to control it. So no harm is done. Another is that biological control is better than using chemicals which poison other living things as well as the one it is used against.

WINGLESS INSECTS

Insects have lived on the Earth for a very long time. Scientists can tell from *fossils* that the first insects appeared more than 350 million years ago. When these prehistoric insects died, their bodies were preserved by being turned into rock. By finding out how long ago the rock was made scientists can tell how old are the insects. The first insects were very small. They had three pairs of legs like insects today, but they had no wings. As the millions of years went by some of the insects grew larger. They also began to grow wings. At first their wings were no more than tiny flaps on the thorax. They were probably useless for flying but perhaps they helped the insects to glide through the air when they jumped.

As the wings grew larger the insects could make longer flights. They could also choose where they wanted to go. One of the things they wanted to do was to search for a mate and this was almost certainly the first use to which wings were put. Certainly no insect grows a complete set of wings until it is ready to mate.

There are insects living today that have no wings. They are so small they are hard to see without a magnifying glass. Most of them live in the soil, but there is one that can be seen in houses. This one may be 1 cm ($\frac{3}{8}$ in) long and is known as the silverfish. It is a tiny silvery insect shaped like a miniature fish on legs, with very long antennae. The silverfish is a *bristletail*, one of a group of insects named after the three bristles at the tip of the abdomen.

Springtails are another sort of wingless insect. They are also very small and they live in huge numbers in the soil and elsewhere. Their name comes from the spring-like mechanism which makes them leap into the air when they are disturbed. Bristletails and springtails are the oldest and most primitive insects we know. They are probably something like the very first insects to appear on earth.

With so many insects flying around, especially when the weather is warm, it is easy to think that all insects fly. This is not so. Only adult insects can fly and there are plenty of *species* where the

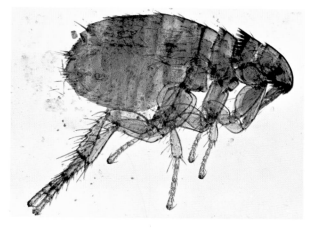

◄Bed bugs, like fleas, have no need of wings. They get an easy living sucking blood from people while they sleep. They were very common when people did not realise the importance of washing regularly and having clean clothes and bed clothes.

▲Fleas live on people and animals. They suck their blood. Their ancestors had wings but lost them when they took up blood-sucking.

adult insects have lost the power of flight. Some flies and moths have lost their wings and there are whole groups of flightless insects.

Among those that never fly at all some are the most troublesome. These are the fleas, lice and bed bugs, which all live by sucking blood. Although they are wingless now, their ancestors had wings millions of years ago.

◄From the study of insect fossils scientists know that the silverfish is like the first insects to appear millions of years ago. It never had wings.

Fleas

Fleas feed on the blood of *mammals* and birds. Their larvae live on the dirt in nests and on hairs and the adults suck the blood of the animals. When an animal approaches, the fleas start to jump in all directions. Those that land on the animal can then suck its blood and then fall off again. Their tough bodies protect them when the animal scratches itself. Each kind of animal has its own kind of flea and only a few fleas can live on more than one kind of animal. Fleas transmit such diseases as myxomatosis and plague.

Lice

There are two kinds of lice. The biting lice are found on birds, and occasionally mammals. They feed on the feathers and pieces of skin. The sucking lice feed on blood. As with the fleas, each kind of louse lives on a particular kind of animal. Three kinds of lice live on human beings. The head louse lays its eggs, or nits, on hairs and the body louse in clothing. It is these lice that carry the disease typhus. The third is the crab louse which lives among hair.

Most booklice live in the Tropics and are found among dead leaves, under bark or in birds' nests. One kind is found in old books where it feeds on the glue in the bindings and on moulds.

◄A rich source of insect fossils is amber, a fossil gum or resin. Pieces of amber often have insects embalmed in them.

21

LIVING LIGHT

▶A tree in Malaya lit up at night by fireflies. The male (**small picture**) flashes first, then the female replies.

In the world of living things there are many thousands of different animals and plants that glow like tiny electric bulbs. Most of them live in the sea; not one is found in fresh water. The smallest are so tiny they can be seen only with a microscope, yet there are so many of them they sometimes light up great areas of the ocean's surface. On land there are several kinds of insect that flash lights at night. They are called fireflies and glowworms.

The surprising thing about these *luminous* insects, as well as all other living things that glow, is that their light is cold. After an electric light bulb has been switched on it soon gets hot. The current flowing through it is a form of energy. The light the bulb gives out is another kind of energy, and the heat from the bulb is a third kind. Only one-tenth of the energy in our electric lighting is used to give light, the rest is wasted in the form of heat. No heat or warmth is given off by the plants or animals that glow.

'Living light', as it has been called, was used by people long before electricity was discovered and long before gaslight was used, or even candles. People living in jungles put these insects in their hair to give light and Chinese scholars used them to read books at night.

Fireflies and glowworms

Fireflies and glowworms are neither flies nor worms. They are beetles. There are about two thousand different kinds, living mainly in the Tropics. The best-known species is the European glowworm.

Usually both male and female have lights and they are used to attract members of the opposite sex. Each species has its own code of signals, based on differences in the length of the interval between flashes. Experimenters have tried flashing electric lights at fireflies and if the time between flashes was right the fireflies replied.

The light organs are like tiny motorcar headlights in various parts of the abdomen, and sometimes in the thorax. The skin over them is transparent, like the lens of a lamp, and there is a layer behind the light which reflects the light. A chemical called luciferin makes the light. The name is from the Latin word 'lucifer', meaning light-bearer. Luciferin glows with a yellowish-green light when mixed with air from the insect's breathing system. The light is not very strong, only one-fortieth of the strength of a candle flame. The colour is, however, one to which the human eye is very sensitive. So fireflies appear very bright. Compared with electric light, which loses so much energy as heat, a firefly's light organ is very efficient. It gives out 95 per cent of its energy as light and only 5 per cent as heat.

The larva of the glowworm also gives off some light and even the eggs give out a little light.

The larvae of the glowworm fly of New Zealand use their glow to attract other insects so they can catch and eat them.

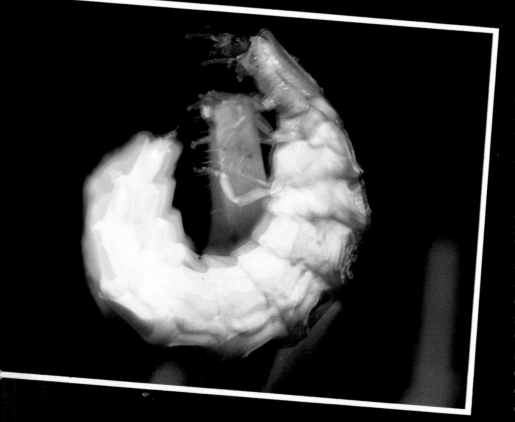

▲A flightless female glowworm clings to a grass stem, her light organ glowing to attract a male.

DRAGONFLIES

A long time ago, when people knew less about natural history than they do today, they used to frighten themselves by inventing animals. One of these terrifying animals was the dragon. This was supposed to be a huge serpent with wings that breathed fire from its nostrils. So it was natural that when they saw a large insect with a long body and wings they should call it a dragonfly. From the way they hunt dragonflies are the hawks among insects. Indeed, in the United States they are called mosquito hawks.

Many dragonflies are beautifully coloured, especially the small ones called damselflies. They have long bodies and two pairs of long, lace-like wings. Some dragonflies are large, with wings 19 cm (7½ in) across. But the largest dragonflies that ever lived measured 70 cm (27½ in) across the wings, although their bodies

were probably very thin. These dragonflies lived 280 million years ago.

Dragonflies have such large eyes that often they cover the whole of the head. Except in small dragonflies, the damselflies, the wings are always held out at right angles to the body. The legs are always held forward, ready to grasp something. This may be the stem of a plant when they need to rest. Or it may be to grasp an insect when feeding.

Dragonfly larvae
Adult dragonflies always live near water and the dragonfly larva lives in water. It has no wings and spends its time crawling over the bottom of a river or lake feeding on other insects or small fishes. To catch its prey it has a curious set of mouth-parts, called a mask. When not hunting the larva folds its mask

▼This larva, or nymph, of an emperor dragonfly has just caught a tadpole. The hooks on the mask grip the prey near its tail.

underneath its face. To catch its prey the larva lies in wait until a small creature comes near it. Then it suddenly shoots out its mask. At the tip of the mask are hooks that open to grasp the prey. The mask is then pulled back. The prey is drawn with it, held by the hooks, and the prey is seized by the jaws.

A new adult emerges

A dragonfly may spend two to three years as a larva, growing slowly bigger. Then, when it is fully grown, it climbs up the stem of a water plant growing out of the water. It hangs by its legs from the stem, resting.

After a time, which may be from 20 minutes to several hours, depending on how hot the weather is, the skin splits down the back and out comes the adult dragonfly. The larger dragonflies leave the water after sunset and are ready to fly before sunrise. The smaller dragonflies may do so during the day.

The newly emerged dragonfly is pale and soft, with glistening crumpled wings. It hangs by its feet from the empty skin it has just left. This allows time for the wings to expand, harden and dry. Once the wings have hardened the dragonfly takes wing and spends the next few days catching insects. Using its large eyes to see them at a distance and its strong wings to fly fast, it grasps its prey with its legs.

The life-cycle continues

After two days or more, again depending on the weather, the dragonfly goes back to water. Each male marks out a territory which it patrols, flying up and down, fighting other males to drive them away.

The females also go back to the water. Each chooses a mate. The male and female then fly tandem for a while. That is, the male embraces the female and the two fly together, one behind the other. Once she has mated the female lays her eggs in water. In some species she merely dips the tip of her abdomen in water to lay one egg at a time. In a few species she may enter the water to lay the eggs on water plants.

▼A dragonfly larva, usually called a nymph, has climbed up the stem of a water plant growing up out of the water. The larval skin has split. The adult dragonfly has climbed out and is hanging from the empty skin to allow its wings to dry.

▼Adult of a large species of dragonfly at rest on an evergreen bush. This shows the long slender body that gave the insect the name of 'devil's needle'. Large dragonflies do not fold their wings over the body when resting.

▲The male (right) and female (left) of this species of damselfly are very different. The female lacks the bright colours and banded wings of the male. Damselflies rest with their wings together above their backs, more like butterflies than dragonflies.

▶An adult damselfly clings to the larval case from which it has just emerged. Its wings are limp at first, but will soon dry and harden and the new adult will be able to fly fast and well.

INSECTS THAT SING

◀The green bush cricket lives among trees and bushes. It rubs the row of spines on its left forewing over the edge of the right forewing to make its 'song'. Each species of grasshopper and bush cricket has its own distinctive song.

▲Most grasshoppers have two pairs of wings. The hind wings are larger than the front wings. When the grasshopper is at rest the hind wings lie folded over the back, under the front wings. The hind wings can be spread during a leap. This increases the distance a grasshopper can cover in one leap.

Plenty of insects make sounds, even if it is only from the buzzing of their wings. There are others that sing, although it would be more correct to say they make instrumental music. These insects are the grasshoppers, crickets and cicadas. There are 6,000 species of grasshopper spread throughout the world, especially in the Tropics.

Grasshoppers belong to the group of insects which have an incomplete metamorphosis (p 15). They have long strong hindlegs that help them jump long distances. Most of them have two pairs of wings. The front pair is stiff but the hind pair are flimsy and fold up like fans to lie under the cover of the front wings. Most grasshoppers cannot fly well and just use their wings to help them glide further when they jump.

Grasshoppers sing by rubbing a hindleg against a forewing. The leg has a row of knobs which makes the wing vibrate. It is rather like running your finger along the teeth of a comb.

You can tell the different species of grasshoppers by their songs, just as you can tell different birds by their songs. Some grasshoppers have special courtship songs. In some species the male also does

▲Before laying her eggs the female cicada makes slits in the bark. Then she lays groups of eggs in each slit.

a dance, moving his body and antennae in time with the song. This attracts the female who comes near to listen. She listens with an ear drum on each side of her abdomen.

►The bush cricket is a short-horned grasshopper. That is, it is a grasshopper with short antennae. This one, singing merrily on the grass, is about to fall victim to the chameleon that has shot out its sticky tongue to make a meal of it.

Singing pets

Crickets look like grasshoppers but they usually sing at night. Crickets also sing in a different way. They rub the hind edge of the left forewing against a row of teeth on the right forewing. The songs of some crickets are quite musical and in China and other parts of Asia crickets are kept in cages as singing pets. Only the males sing and the females have ears on the forelegs to listen to them.

What was it Katy did?

A third kind of insect musician is the bush cricket. It looks like a grasshopper but has long whip-like antennae. It sings in the same way as the crickets except that it rubs the hind edge of the right forewing against a row of teeth on the left forewing. Its songs are always high pitched, often beyond our hearing, but sometimes almost deafeningly loud.

There is a bush cricket in the United States that is known as the katydid. This is because it rasps out the words 'Katy did, Katy did'.

As with grasshoppers, the songs of bush crickets can be used to tell what species is singing. Their songs differ slightly according to the weather. The higher the temperature, the more rapid the calls.

Singing cicadas

Cicadas are related to aphids and not to grasshoppers and crickets at all. They also sing in a different way. On the underside of the abdomen, near where it joins the thorax, there is a pair of sound chambers like drums. The 'skin' of the drum vibrates rapidly to make loud calls. These are usually very shrill, but in Peru there is a cicada that makes a sound like a railway engine in the distance. An Egyptian cicada makes a sound like a bell and a Greek cicada sounds like a harp.

▼Two different ways in which insects make their 'music'. **Left** The male cicada pulls in part of its abdomen, the drum, then lets it flap back. By doing this very fast it makes its song, which can be heard for quite a distance. **Below** The grasshopper has a row of tiny knobs on its hind legs (magnified **right**) which it rubs on the edge of its front wings to make its song.

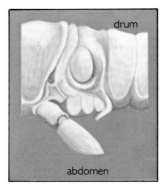

drum

abdomen

knobs on inner surface of hind leg

the knobs highly magnified

APHIDS OR PLANT LICE

Aphids are also known as plant lice, but are tiny bugs that multiply at a surprising rate. They can do a great deal of damage to crops both by sucking the sap from them and by infecting them with virus diseases. The gardener who sees them in large numbers on his roses calls them greenfly. The farmer who sees aphids on his bean crops calls them blackfly.

The largest aphids are little more than 5 mm ($\frac{1}{4}$ in) long and most are not more than 2–3 mm ($\frac{1}{8}$ in) long. Their bodies are soft, oval in shape with small heads and long antennae. On the underside of the head is a beak to pierce the skin of plants and suck sap.

Gardeners are often surprised to see their favourite plants covered with aphids when a day or two before there were none. They are puzzled to know where they come from. The answer lies in the aphids' life-cycle.

At the end of the summer aphids lay their eggs in the cracks in the bark of trees. The following spring only females hatch from the eggs. These females are wingless, so they stay on the plant where they hatched. Each one pushes her beak into the plant and begins sucking sap. At the same time she has her first baby.

The mother goes on feeding as one baby after another appears from the tip of her abdomen. At first the baby is no more than a tiny sausage-shaped body. Then its legs and antennae unfold as it drops onto the surface of the leaf. Soon it pushes its beak into the skin of the plant and begins to feed.

In the next 24 hours another 24 baby aphids will be born to the same mother. The next day the same thing will happen, and the day after. What is more, in a week's time each of the babies will have grown and started having its own babies, at the rate of one an hour. All these will be females, too.

Every now and then, a generation of females with wings appears. They fly to new plants and that is why aphids suddenly appear in the garden. In the autumn male aphids are born. They mate with the females who then lay eggs which survive the winter and hatch in spring and so the life-cycle continues.

It has been estimated that if all the offspring from a single mother survived there would be in one year enough to equal the weight of 500,000,000 men. This does not happen, of course, because aphids have many enemies. Small birds eat them, so do ladybirds and their larvae. There are several other kinds of insects or insect larvae that eat nothing but aphids. A tiny wasp, itself hardly bigger than an aphid, lays its eggs in them. The larvae from the wasp's eggs feed on the insides of the aphids leaving only dried husks.

Ants and aphids

An aphid spends its life sucking sap from a plant. This sap contains water, sugar and protein. The amount of protein in the sap is very small so the aphid must take

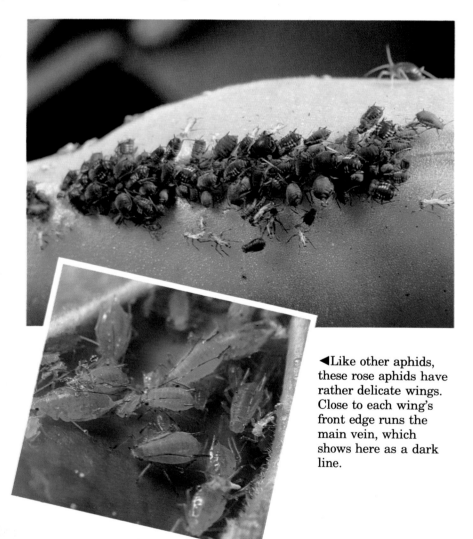

▼Blackfly, black blight or black bean aphids are just three of the names given to these aphids. In summer they live in broad beans, sugar beet, spinach and dock plants.

◄Like other aphids, these rose aphids have rather delicate wings. Close to each wing's front edge runs the main vein, which shows here as a dark line.

in large quantities of the liquid to obtain enough protein. The rest is given out as a sweet liquid, known as *honeydew*. Ants are very fond of honeydew. Wherever there are aphids on plants you will see ants visiting them to collect the honeydew.

Some ants go further and look after aphids in order to milk them. The ants protect the aphids from their enemies, and some ants even take the aphids into their own nests for better protection.

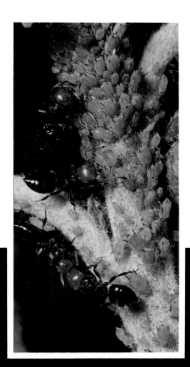

▶Ants and aphids living together on the stem of a plant that already shows signs of withering. The ants feed on the honeydew which aphids give out, so they protect the aphids from predators.

▲Aphids of several ages but all are females. For most of their lives aphids are busy giving birth to babies even when there are no males around. The one on the left is giving birth. The baby can be seen leaving her body.

▶Fortunately for the farmer and the gardener aphids have many enemies. Here a ladybird is eating its way through a crowd of aphids.

TERMITES

A diet of wood

There are billions upon billions of insects in the world that feed on wood. They are called termites. They can eat wood because they have colonies of microscopic single-celled animals in their stomachs. These animals are called *flagellates* and they turn indigestible wood into food the termites can digest. Termites are sometimes called white ants because they look like ants but are colourless. Like

▶A termitarium, the home of a colony of termites. Although made of earth and saliva the outer crust is so hard a pickaxe is needed to break it. Some termitaria are known to be a hundred years old.

ants, they live in colonies and swarm in large numbers.

Termites live mainly in the forests and grasslands of the tropics, although some live in France and southern Canada. Their main food, too, is wood. When trees die, the termites set to work on them. Without the termites these dead trees would rot only very slowly. The action of the termites helps clear the ground for new plants and trees to grow.

A diet of wood means that nothing made of wood is safe from termites. They eat telegraph poles, furniture and books. In countries where termites live it is always a problem how to keep such things safe from them. They also eat the straw out of mud bricks and even attack plastics. A few kinds of termite do not use flagellates to digest wood. Instead they build special fungus gardens in their nests. The termites chew up plants and let fungus grow on them. Then they eat the fungus.

Air-conditioned homes

There are 2,000 different species, or kinds, of termite. Some form only small colonies. They live in logs or in tunnels they make in the ground. By far the best known are those that live in big colonies. They build huge homes of earth known as termitaria. These termites are found in parts of Africa, southern Asia, and Australia where the largest termitaria are found. These may be 6m (20ft) high.

A termitarium is made of tiny pellets of earth placed like bricks and cemented together with saliva and the termites' own droppings. The walls are so hard that it is difficult to break them open with a pick-axe. Inside there is a maze of rooms and passages all with perfect air-conditioning so the inside always has the same temperature and humidity.

Different jobs for different termites

Each colony of termites consists of several groups or castes. There is a queen and a king that are responsible for producing the many generations of workers needed to do the work of the colony. Unlike ants and bees, the king does not die after mating but lives with the queen in the nest. There are also some junior queens and kings. These do not breed but should anything happen to the reigning queen or king one of them takes their place.

The reigning queen has an enormous abdomen, filled with eggs. She spends her time laying eggs. One queen was seen to lay 36,000 in twenty-four hours. The queen spends her life in a chamber at the centre of a termitarium. She cannot move about and has to be fed and kept clean by the workers, who also carry away and look after the eggs.

As well as workers there are soldier termites with big heads armed with large jaws. Some soldiers squirt a sticky fluid at enemies such as ants.

The workers and soldiers do not live very long. The workers must look after the eggs and larvae, build and repair the termitarium and gather food. They also gather water. Termites need water and a moist atmosphere in which to live. Those that live in deserts sink shafts 30 m (100 ft) in the sand. There is a constant procession of workers up and down these shafts. Each worker carries a drop of water to supply the nest and keep it moist.

When the workers go out collecting food they avoid the light. If they cannot burrow through soil or wood they build

tunnels of earth over the surface of the ground and up tree trunks. Wherever they go they are guarded by the soldiers.

Worker and soldier termites are wingless, but every so often swarms of winged termites leave the colony. These are the young queens and kings. After flying around for a while they come down to earth and shed their wings. Then, they crawl about over the ground in pairs seeking places to build new colonies.

▶This is not a caterpillar – it is a queen termite. The whitish sausage is her abdomen swollen by all the eggs she will lay, about 10,000 a day! Beside her is the king termite.

▼Some soldier termites can squirt a sticky liquid at enemy insects. All soldier termites have large heads. As they move about inside the termitarium their heads knock against the walls. This makes a drumming sound. Scientists thought this was an alarm system, but all termites do it. It is only the soldiers, with their large heads, that we can hear.

▶The huge queen termite at the centre of the termitarium. She is surrounded by workers that feed her, keep her clean and remove the eggs as she lays them.

BUTTERFLIES AND MOTHS

▲The bright 'eye' markings on the wings of a peacock butterfly help protect it. A predator attacking the butterfly strikes at the 'eyes' and not at the body.

Butterflies and moths come in all sorts of shapes, sizes and colours. The smallest are only a few millimetres long, about the size of a grain of wheat or rice. The largest, the bird's wing butterfly from south-east Asia, is about 14 cm (nearly 6 in) across its wings. There are at least 150,000 different kinds, most of which are moths. In fact, in most parts of the world moths out-number butterflies by 20 to 1.

Is it a butterfly or a moth?
Butterflies and moths are easy to recognise. But what are the differences between them?

If you can get close enough the best way to tell if it is a butterfly or a moth is to look at the antennae. The antennae of butterflies always end in a knob. Moths' antennae are usually small and come in different shapes.

If you cannot get close enough to see the antennae on the head, look how the insect folds its wings when resting. A moth folds its wings across its back. A butterfly brings its wings together above its back.

Mostly butterflies are larger than moths but the hawk moths are nearly as big as the largest butterflies. Butterflies are usually more brightly coloured than moths, although there are some colourful moths. Butterflies tend to fly by day,

moths by night. But there are also many moths that fly by day.

Scales of many shades
If you touch the wing of a butterfly or moth, however gently, you find you have fine specks of dust on your fingers. This dust is made up of the tiny scales that cover the wings. In fact, the scientific name for butterflies and moths is Lepidoptera, meaning scaly wings. These scales, arranged on the wings like tiles on a roof, give these insects their colours in two different ways. Mostly, the colours in a butterfly's wings are due to *pigments*, or colouring matter. But the scales are also of different shapes and so reflect light in different ways. This often gives rise to other sets of colours.

The colours of the wings are important. In most Lepidoptera they help to camouflage the insect and make it hard to find. Others, like the burnet moth, use their colours to make themselves as obvious as possible. These colours are known as warning colours because they warn birds that the insect has a nasty taste. Once a bird has tried to eat one of these butterflies or moths, it will never touch another.

Moths and butterflies lay their eggs on the leaves which the larvae, called caterpillars, will eat. Each kind has its favourite kind of plant. White butterflies like to eat the leaves of cabbages and related plants; privet hawk moth caterpillars live on privet and lilac. The caterpillar of the clothes moth is unusual because it eats wool.

Caterpillars do little more than eat. Often they stop only to shed their skins. Where caterpillars are very numerous they may completely strip trees of their leaves. But caterpillars have many enemies, and are eaten by birds and other animals. Many caterpillars protect themselves by camouflage or by showing with warning colours that they are unpleasant to eat, just as some adults do.

When a caterpillar is fully grown, it finds a suitable place to pupate and become an adult. The *pupa* of a butterfly forms a hard case called a chrysalis. Most

►A tortoiseshell butterfly resting in the sunshine, showing its clubbed antennae and brightly coloured wings.

►Although these two butterflies look so different, they are both common blues. Many kinds of butterfly have colour variations like this, which makes them hard to identify.

►The distinctive tail gives this butterfly its name – swallowtail.

▼Burnet moths are unusual – they have club antennae like butterflies.

►The pine hawk moth uses camouflage to protect itself. The colour of its wings looks very like the bark of the pine trees on which it is resting.

moths pupate inside a cocoon of silk.

Adult moths and butterflies feed by sipping nectar from flowers with a long tubular tongue or *proboscis*. They usually live only for a short time, but some hibernate for the winter or, like the American monarch butterfly, migrate south to warm countries.

▲The long 'tails' of the Indian moon moth are really part of the hind wings.

►The *Kallima* butterfly of south-east Asia looks like a dead leaf to protect itself from its enemies.

►The colour and 'tails' of the puss moth caterpillar are warnings to its enemies. It can also squirt acid at anything attacking it.

TWO-WINGED FLIES

▶This bluebottle fly is a close relative of the housefly. Both are two-winged flies; both are a nuisance. They crawl over food and leave behind germs. The bluebottle lays its eggs in the dead bodies of small animals. The maggots from the eggs feed on this dead meat.

All sorts of insects are called flies but to the scientist the word 'fly' means two-winged flies only. That is, true flies such as houseflies, bluebottles, mosquitoes, midges and craneflies. All these have one pair of wings. Their hind wings have become transformed into *halteres*.

Halteres are small knobs on stalks that act as balancing organs. They vibrate in time with the wings and they work like the gyroscopic compass of an aeroplane, telling the fly of any change in its direction of flight. The halteres on the cranefly or daddy-long-legs are quite easy to see.

True flies are found all over the world, from the Arctic to the Equator and down to the Antarctic continent. They are found on the tops of high mountains and in caves and mines deep underground. The largest, the robber flies, live in the Tropics. They are 7.5 cm (3 in) long and measure 10 cm (4 in) across the spread wings. In contrast the smallest flies are little more than 1 millimetre ($\frac{1}{25}$ in) long.

In Alaska, northern Canada and northern Europe, the swarms of mosquitoes, horseflies and blackflies are unbearable during the short Arctic summer. In the Tropics these swarms are found mainly in the tops of tall trees, where they make life uncomfortable for monkeys.

Many two-winged flies breed in water or where it is damp. They can feed on many kinds of food, especially the garbage we leave lying around. The housefly, for example, becomes rare where people use packaged foods.

The best known of the true flies is the housefly. It was not found in America until 1952, but has increased rapidly there since then. Another well-known fly is the cranefly or daddy-long-legs. Its larvae are called leather jackets. They live in damp ground feeding on the roots of grass, doing much damage to pasture land.

The life-cycle of a fly

Most two-winged flies pass through four stages during their lives: the egg, larva, pupa and adult. This is usual in insects, but some flies shorten this. The eggs of some blowflies hatch inside the body of the female, who then gives birth to larvae. Tsetse flies do the same except that they do not drop their larvae until these are about to turn into pupae.

Destructive flies

Two-winged flies can spread disease. Blackflies carry tiny worms that can cause blindness in people. The housefly spreads diseases of the skin and the intestine.

Many kinds of two-winged flies also cause damage to crops. There are many kinds of fruit fly, as well as the onion fly and the cabbage root fly.

▶Hoverflies are living helicopters. They can hang motionless in the air or dart this way and that. They are often mistaken for bees and other stinging insects.

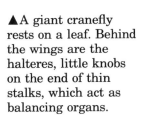

▲A giant cranefly
rests on a leaf. Behind
the wings are the
halteres, little knobs
on the end of thin
stalks, which act as
balancing organs.

BEES

On a sunny day in summer any patch of flowers will be alive with insects, especially bees. They will be busy collecting nectar and pollen from the flowers. There are many kinds of bees. The largest are the bumblebees, but you are most likely to see honeybees.

Honeybees

Honeybees live in colonies, in hollow trees and in hives. They are useful because they pollinate flowers so that they produce seeds and fruit. They also make honey to feed their larvae and as a food supply for the winter.

▶The larva of a queen bee developing inside a cell in the part of the honeycomb reserved for eggs and larvae.

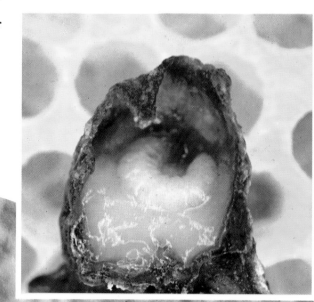

Each colony contains one queen, a few hundred males called drones, and as many as sixty thousand workers. The queen is the largest of the three types of bee. Her task is to lay 1,500 eggs each day. The workers are females that cannot lay eggs. Instead, they do all the work of the hive.

Inside the hive, or the nest, is the honeycomb. This is made of wax. The workers give out the wax in flakes from glands between the joints of their abdomens. They chew it until it is soft, then build it into a comb made up of six-sided cells. One part of the comb contains eggs and larvae. Other parts are filled with honey.

When the queen is ready to lay her eggs she crawls over the comb, pushes her abdomen into a cell and lays an egg, one in each cell. Three days later a grub, or larva, hatches from the egg. It is fed and tended by the workers. At first it is fed on royal jelly, a special saliva produced by the workers. Then it is fed on honey. A larva that is fed only on royal jelly grows into a queen.

When a worker first leaves its cell it is fed by other workers, but soon it starts to feed itself. A young worker's first task is to feed newly hatched larvae with honey from the comb. The worker's next job is to

◀Section through a plant stem showing the nest of a solitary bee. The larvae are surrounded by yellow pollen, which the female has put there as food for them.

repair the old comb and the walls of the nest. The comb is repaired with wax but the nest is repaired with bee glue, known as propolis. This is made from the sap of certain trees, including poplar. The bee has to make short flights from the hive to get this. In doing so it learns its way about. Young workers also help clean the hive, look after the queen and defend the hive.

▲These worker bees are busy on a honeycomb. In the summer, when bees are most active, each worker only lives for a few weeks.

▶A swarm of honeybees resting on a tree before flying off in search of a sheltered place to build a new nest.

When it is three weeks old a worker is ready to go out and collect nectar and pollen. Foraging workers use their keen senses of smell and sight to find the flowers with the best supply of nectar. When a bee has found a good supply of nectar, it tells the other workers by dancing on the comb. The way it dances tells them in which direction to go and how far to fly.

▲A new worker bee emerges from its cell in the comb. It will work inside the nest for three weeks, until ready to collect pollen and nectar.

▶The male bees, or drones, are not as big as the queen bee, although they are larger than the worker bees.

◄Most bees are solitary, they do not live in large groups in hives. This solitary bee has full yellow pollen sacs each side of its body.

▼Each hive of honeybees can only have one queen. If there is more than one they will fight, each one trying to sting the other to death.

Bumblebees

Bumblebees also live in nests containing a queen and workers, but the nests are smaller and there are fewer workers. Unlike honeybees, all bumblebees die in the winter, except for the young queens which hibernate and start new nests in the spring.

Solitary bees

Honeybees and bumblebees are unusual because they live in groups. Most of the 19,000 kinds of bee we know lead solitary lives. The female lays her eggs in a burrow in the ground or in a plant stem. Each egg is placed on a lump of pollen moistened with nectar, so that the larva will have plenty of food when it hatches.

▲A bumblebee collecting nectar and pollen. The pollen collects on the hairs of its body, but it uses its long, tube-like tongue to get the nectar.

◄The carpenter bee gets its name because it can eat through wood with its strong mouthparts. But it still needs flowers for food.

43

WASPS

▶Inside the wasps' nest are cells, also made of paper, in which the queen lays her eggs. Grubs hatch from the eggs and are fed by the workers. Here an adult wasp, having pupated, has now become fully grown and is leaving its cell.

Wasps have a bad name. There are two reasons for this: they can sting and they like sweet fruits and can damage crops. They do have a good side, because they feed their larvae on other troublesome insects, such as bluebottle flies.

There are 20,000 different kinds of wasp. They are of two kinds, solitary wasps and social wasps. Solitary wasps are usually small and are often brilliantly coloured red, blue or green. Social wasps are the ones with yellow and black bodies. They are sometimes called yellow jackets. The black and yellow bands warn birds and other insect-eating animals that the wasps are dangerous.

Social wasps

Social wasps build large nests of paper. In each nest there is one queen which is larger than the other wasps. There are several male wasps and the rest are workers.

At the end of the year all the wasps die except for a few new queens. These spend the winter asleep and in the following spring each one starts a new nest.

Some kinds of wasp build their nests in the twiggy branches of a tree, in hollow tree trunks, or in the roofs of buildings. Others build them in the ground. A queen who builds in the earth either finds a mouse-hole or else digs a hole of her own, carrying away the earth a few grains at a time. The queen then looks for some dead wood. This may be a dead tree branch or a wooden post. She chews off small pieces of dead wood with her strong jaws. She carries each piece back

to where the nest will be and chews it thoroughly. It mixes with her saliva to make a paste, which sets to form a sort of 'paper'.

With this 'paper' she makes a group of cup-shaped cells, and then lays an egg in each one. When a larva hatches she feeds it with insects. After the larvae are fully grown they change into pupae. Very soon an adult wasp comes out and begins its life as a worker.

The queen wasp is then able to spend her whole time laying eggs. As more workers appear, they make the nest bigger. The bigger the nest the more eggs the queen can lay, and the more worker wasps there are to catch insects to feed the larvae.

On warm sunny days insects of all kinds settle on flowers to feed and sun themselves. Suddenly a wasp lands on a bluebottle, holding it prisoner. The wasp bites off the bluebottle's wings, then each of its legs, leaving only the body. Clasping the body of the fly in its legs, the wasp carries it back to the nest, to feed the wasp larvae.

Like many adult insects, the adult wasps eat little or nothing. They take only sweet things, such as ripe fruit and nectar. They also come indoors if there is jam or honey about.

In late summer the queen wasp lays fewer eggs so there is less work for the worker wasps to do. As autumn draws on the workers die off, so does the old queen. Finally, only new queens and the males are left. We can tell the males by their long antennae. Queens and males mate and then the males die. The queens look for sheltered places in which to spend the winter, perhaps a hollow tree or under the roof of a house. In spring the queens emerge to build a nest and start a new colony.

Solitary wasps

Solitary wasps do not have workers. The female wasp builds a small nest, sometimes in the ground or in a crevice in a wall or post. She then searches for a caterpillar or spider and paralyses it with her sting. She carries it to her nest and

▼Wasps build nests of paper which they make by chewing wood. Most wasps' nests are tucked away somewhere out of sight. Tree wasps build their nests among the small branches of shrubs and trees.

▶The most dreaded of the wasp family is the hornet. It is larger than other wasps yet for all that is harmless if not disturbed.

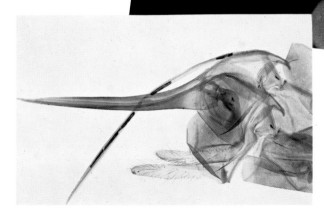

◀The hind end of a wasp, photographed under a microscope, showing the sting.

lays her eggs by it. When the wasp larvae hatch out, they have a supply of fresh food. The female wasp leaves enough food when she lays her eggs and does not return to the nest.

Many other solitary wasps do not make a nest but lay their eggs in the bodies of living caterpillars and other small animals. When the wasp larvae hatch out they begin to feed on the body of the caterpillar but without killing it. The unfortunate caterpillar goes on living until the larvae are fully grown and ready to turn into pupae.

▶You often have to look closely at an insect to say what kind it is but there is little doubt about wasps. They buzz loudly and their yellow and black bodies are a warning of the painful sting.

ANTS

▲ Like all queen ants, the queen fire ant is the largest ant in the colony and the most important, because it is she who lays the eggs from which new members of the colony will hatch.

▼ Section through an ants' nest. Although the anthill above ground is large, there is actually more of the nest underground.

There are 8,000 different kinds of ant in the world. They are most numerous in the warmer countries. Ants all look much alike except in size and they all have a narrow 'waist' between the thorax and abdomen. They have strong jaws too, and an ant's bite can be painful. They can also sting, and the wood ant squirts *formic acid* from the end of its abdomen at its enemies.

Queens, workers and males

All ants live in colonies in which there may be as many as 100,000 ants. There is one queen, who spends all her time laying eggs, and a few males. At certain times of the year the males leave the nest and take to the air. The young queens follow them and each mates with a male. After mating, the queens fly down again, tear off their wings and start to build a

nest. They may live for 15 years. The males die soon after mating.

All the rest of the ants in a nest are workers, which are females that cannot lay eggs. They have no wings and they do all the work. They build the nest and keep it clean. They look after the eggs and the young larvae, and they gather food.

If you find an ants' nest, you will probably see streams of ants walking to and fro along a trail. As the trail gets farther from the nest, there will be fewer ants on it because they spread out to look for food. You can sometimes see the returning ants carrying food in their jaws.

The ants find their way back to the nest either by following trails of scent laid by other ants, or by using the sun as a compass.

Different species of ant have different kinds of food. It may be seeds, dead animals or plants. Wood ants eat living animals. Leaf-cutter ants cut pieces of leaves, take them to the nest and grow tiny fungi on them to eat. Some ants feed on the sugary fluids given out by greenfly (p 31).

Different kinds of ant

Army ants move about the country in columns eating any animal they come across, even large animals if they cannot get out of the way. At night they all come together in a ball to rest under a log or other sheltered place. The next day they set off again. When the queen is ready to lay some eggs, the ants settle in a hole for several days, waiting for the eggs to hatch and the larvae to become new workers.

There are several species of slave-making ants who use other kinds of ant to help look after their nests and find food. Bright red robber ants raid the nests of black ants and carry off their pupae. When the black ants emerge from the pupae they work in their new homes. Amazon ants have such huge jaws that they cannot collect their own food. They can only survive by making slaves of other ants.

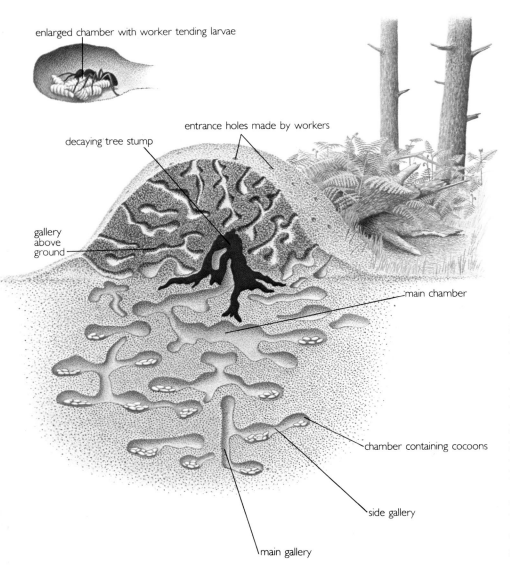

enlarged chamber with worker tending larvae

entrance holes made by workers

decaying tree stump

gallery above ground

main chamber

chamber containing cocoons

side gallery

main gallery

►Cross-section through an underground ants' nest. The white objects are the pupae, usually called ants' eggs.

▼These are the mouth parts of a safari ant. There are thousands of ants in a swarm, so you can imagine the damage they can do.

►These South African safari ants have raided a termites' nest, and are carrying away some of their victims. These ants can kill and eat almost any living thing in their path if it does not run away fast enough.

►Another kind of ant sews leaves together to make its nest. Worker ants cooperate to pull the leaves of a plant together. When the edges are close one worker carries a larva backwards and forwards across the edges so that the larva's silk 'sews' the leaf edges together. The final nest is a round ball of leaves.

BEETLES

▼The anatomy of a stag beetle. The left wing cover is in place, but the other is shown forward, as it is when the insect is flying.

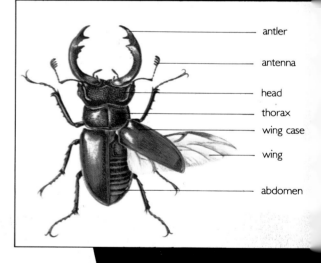

antler

antenna

head

thorax

wing case

wing

abdomen

▲The great diving beetle spends the whole of its life in ponds or streams, preying on smaller animals or even those, such as fishes, larger than itself.

There are 300,000 different kinds of beetles, so there are more beetles than any other kind of insect. The smallest are the feather-wing beetles that measure only 0.04 cm ($\frac{1}{60}$ in) long. The largest are the rhinoceros beetle, goliath beetle and elephant beetle. These may grow up to 16 cm ($6\frac{1}{4}$ in) long. But large or small, all beetles have the same life history. The eggs hatch out into the larvae or grubs which look like small worms. Some beetles stay as larvae for several years before pupating and becoming adults.

Is it a beetle?

There are two things to look out for when you want to identify a beetle. First, a beetle has heavy 'armour' for protection. Beetles are the most heavily armoured of all insects. Second, the front wings are not wings at all, they are hard cases which cover the delicate hind wings when

▼Stored crops may be destroyed by insects. The grain weevil larva grows in a wheat grain (left) becomes a pupa (centre) then the adult bites its way out of the grain (right).

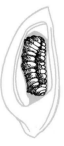 

►The death watch beetle can be a menace in old buildings, boring holes in woodwork and weakening the structure, which may then collapse.

▲The burying beetle does a useful service by burying small dead creatures that it needs for food. In the soil the rest of the buried animal decays and the soil is enriched.

◄The mouth-parts of a weevil. These are highly developed and are used not just for eating but also for drilling holes into plant seeds to lay its eggs in them.

▶The stag beetle takes its name from the large antler-like mandibles of the male.

▼Scarab beetles were regarded as sacred by the Ancient Egyptians.

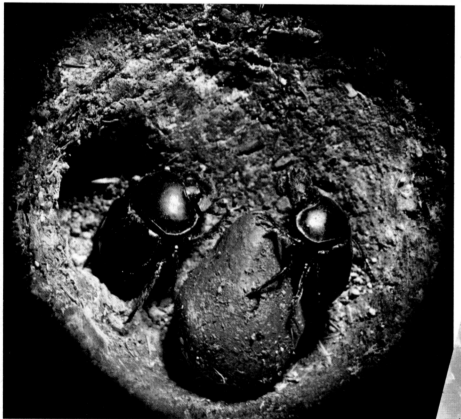

the beetle is not flying.

Most beetles live on the ground or just below its surface, but the ground can be anywhere in the world. There are beetles that live in deserts, in caves and on the seashore. Other kinds of beetle live in the nests of birds, ants and termites, while others live on plants. Again, whether the plants are in tropical forests or on cold mountain slopes, there will probably be some kind of beetle that lives on them. The sea is the only place where no beetles live, although there are kinds that live in rivers, streams and lakes. Beetles that live in water have flattened legs they use as paddles for swimming.

A great variety of foods

The food beetles eat is as varied as the different places in which they live. Most beetles eat plant foods. Weevils eat all the parts of a plant. Leaf beetles feed on the soft parts of the leaves. Wireworms, the larvae of click beetles, eat only roots, as do chafer beetles. Some large beetles drink only nectar. Many small beetles eat only toadstools.

Flesh-eating beetles include ladybirds which eat greenfly and chequered beetles which hunt for bark beetles. Burying beetles, sometimes called sexton beetles, eat only animals that are already dead. The smell of a small dead bird or a dead mouse lying on the ground attracts the

◀This strange beetle was found for the first time in a grotto at Postojna in Yugoslavia. It is only one of many unusual insects found in caves.

burying beetles. Five or six of them land near it and begin carrying away small pieces of earth from under it. Slowly the dead animal sinks into the ground. The female beetles lay their eggs on the body, so when the larvae hatch from the eggs they have a good supply of food.

Dung beetles get their name because they feed on dung. They collect dung and roll it into a ball. Then they push it away, dig a hole in the ground and push it in. There they can feed on it in safety. The scarab, a beetle the Ancient Egyptians admired, is a dung beetle.

▲The ladybird beetle does much good by feeding on the destructive aphids. For this reason nobody ever kills a ladybird.

◄The Colorado beetle of America feeds on plants of the potato family and can destroy potato crops. Sometimes it gets carried to Europe in a ship's cargo. This is serious because it could destroy crops here. You sometimes see warning notices about these beetles outside police stations.

51

INSECT RELATIVES

CRUSTACEANS

All insects belong to the large group of animals called *arthropods*. The name means 'jointed legs'. Spiders, scorpions, centipedes and millipedes are all arthropods too. So are crabs and lobsters, shrimps and prawns and a host of small animals that live in the sea and in fresh water. The largest crab in the world is the Japanese giant crab which is 3 m (10 ft) across its long jointed legs. The smallest water fleas are only 0.25 mm (one-hundredth of an inch).

Food for whales

Tiny crustaceans that bounce up and down in the water of ponds and lakes are called water fleas. They are one of many kinds of small crustaceans which are important food for fishes and other animals. For example, the small prawns called krill exist in such vast numbers that the giant whales can feed on them and nothing else. In fact there are so many kinds of crustacean living in the sea that they are sometimes called 'Insects of the Sea'.

A permanent home

Barnacles look like limpets because they live inside a hard shell and cling firmly to rocks, but they are really crustaceans. Like many other crustaceans they start life as larvae which swim in the sea. When each larva is ready to change into an adult it finds a suitable rock, the bottom of a ship, or even a whale, and glues itself down by its head. It then grows its shell and never moves again. It feeds by sweeping its feathery legs through the water to collect tiny particles of food.

► A water flea one millimetre (0.04 in) long that is found in ponds and lakes in large numbers. It swims by flicking its long antennae.

◄ The blue prawn can change its colour according to the seaweed surrounding it. Among green seaweed it is green, among brown it looks brown and among red it is red. At night it is blue.

▲ The banded coral shrimp, as its name suggests, lives among coral reefs in tropical seas.

▲These tiny crustaceans are called amphipods. They swim on their sides. They live in fresh or saltwater, scavenging dead animal and plant matter for food. They, in turn, become food for larger creatures.

▲Giant prawns like these live in warm seas. Some prawns living in tropical seas can reach 25 cm (10 in) in length. Prawns and shrimps have many enemies besides man. One of the most dangerous ones is the cuttlefish.

►A group of spiny lobsters 'marching' across the seafloor. They belong to the group of crustaceans known as *decapods* – ten legs.

Decapods – living with ten legs

The crabs, lobsters, crayfish and shrimps belong to a group of crustaceans called *decapods*, a word meaning 'ten-legs'. They have eight legs for walking and two which are armed with large claws for feeding and for defence. Many of these animals are important as food. Most live in the sea but crayfish and some crabs and shrimps live in fresh water.

Lobsters and shrimps have a long abdomen with several pairs of swimming legs called swimmerets. But to escape from danger they flick their abdomens forward and shoot away backwards.

Crabs have heavy shells and rarely swim. The abdomen is tucked under the shell and the crab runs sideways on its eight walking legs. One kind of crab, the swimming crab, does swim. Its last pair of legs are flattened and form paddles.

Hermit crabs are rather different from other crabs because they do not have shells of their own. Instead they live in the empty shells of whelks, winkles, or other shellfish. As they grow, hermit crabs grow out of these shells and have to find larger ones. Hermit crabs are in

▲The fiddler crab has compound eyes on movable stalks, so it can see well in all directions. When it buries itself in the sand for protection, it raises its eyes like periscopes to look around.

▶A hermit crab using a whelk's shell for shelter and protection. The strong, well protected claws remain outside the shell, but the rest of the body has no natural protection, which is why the crab needs another creature's empty shell for protection.

great danger as they change shells because they have nothing to protect their soft bodies.

Land crustaceans
By contrast, very few crustaceans are found on land. In West Africa, the Caribbean and the Pacific, there are land crabs. These are crabs that live and feed on land but lay their eggs in the sea. The robber crab of the Pacific grows to 45 cm (18 in) long and can climb trees. The best known land crustaceans are the woodlice or sow bugs. Although woodlice never enter water, they have to live in damp places or they will dry up. They hide in crevices by day and come out to feed at night. Sea slaters, which are relatives of the woodlice, live on seaside beaches.

▲A common shore crab: its abdomen is tucked underneath the body. It has five pairs of legs and a pair of strong pincers.

The squat lobster is a member of the group of animals called crustaceans which includes shrimps and crabs. Crustaceans do not have bones. They have a hard 'skin' as a skeleton on the outside of the body. This is called an exoskeleton. It is made in segments, so that the animal can move around, which it could not do if it was rigid.

▼Unlike most kinds of lobster, the spiny lobster does not have large pinching claws. But the strong spines on the body and antennae act as effective weapons against attackers.

SPIDERS

▶Diagram through a spider's body.

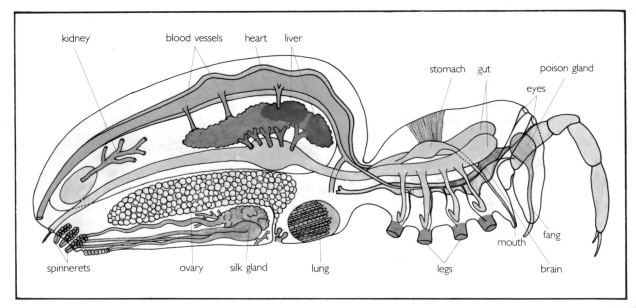

kidney   blood vessels   heart   liver   stomach   gut   poison gland   eyes   fang   mouth   brain   legs   lung   silk gland   ovary   spinnerets

▲A cocoon of silk woven by a female spider for her eggs. She made it in the same way as the wolf spider (**opposite**) made hers, but this egg sac hangs from a web.

◀ Close-up of a spider's spinnerets showing the silk being spun. Each thread in a spider's web is made up of many strands.

▼A wolf spider about to eat a caterpillar it has just caught.

There are 40,000 kinds of spider in the world. Some are barely the size of a pin head. The largest are the hairy bird-eating spiders of South America, nearly as big as your hand. They kill small birds, such as hummingbirds, and are usually referred to as tarantulas.

A spider cannot bite or chew. So, through its hollow fangs it injects digestive juices into the body of the insect it has captured. These turn the inside of the insect's body into a liquid which the spider then sucks up. Except for those that kill birds, spiders feed on insects.

Spiders look like insects (p 6) but instead of having three pairs of legs they have four pairs. A spider also has only two parts to the body, a *prosoma* in front and an abdomen. The prosoma is made

up of the head and the legs. It also bears the mouth with its fangs and, usually, eight eyes in two rows of four each.

Spiders' silk
At the rear end of the abdomen is a group of *spinnerets*. Each spinneret is like a teat that squirts silk in very fine threads. The silk has several uses, of which the spider's web is the commonest.

Most spiders spin a web to catch their prey. This may be an orb web, like that of a garden spider, or a sheet web, like that of a house spider. There is a South African spider that spins a small net and throws it over an insect. Another spider spins a thread weighted with a ball of silk. It swings the ball and throws it over an insect, trapping it.

Not all spiders catch their prey with webs or nets. Wolf spiders stalk insects and jumping spiders leap on their prey. Although neither spins a web, both lay down a dragline as they go, to act as a life-line.

Web-spinners use a dragline, too. One end is fastened to the web. When an insect flies into the web its struggles set up vibrations. The spider feels these through its dragline and comes out to wrap the insect in silk to imprison it, after stabbing it with its fangs to poison it.

Female spiders also use the silk to make cocoons in which to lay their eggs. Unlike most spiders a female wolf spider carries her cocoon around with her, fastened to the tip of her abdomen.

▼A large tropical spider in its web. Some large spiders can spin webs several feet across.

▼To make her egg sacs this spider spins a silk sheet, lays her eggs on it, covers them with more silk and wraps it into a ball.

MILLIPEDES AND CENTIPEDES

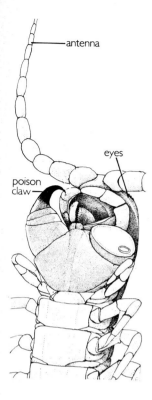

antenna

eyes

poison claw

▲Drawing of the centipede's mouth-parts. On each side of the mouth is a black-tipped poison claw. This first pair of legs stuns or kills the prey before it is eaten.

▼Photograph of the mouth-parts of a centipede.

►Close-up of the underneath of a millipede to show the legs. Each segment of the body has two pairs of legs. But even so, millipedes move quite slowly.

Millipedes and centipedes are arthropods (meaning jointed legs) and so they are distant relatives of crustaceans, spiders and insects. Although millipedes and centipedes look alike they are very different.

The name 'millipede' means a thousand legs. No millipede has that many legs, a few hundred would be nearer the truth. 'Centipede' means a hundred legs. Most centipedes have fifty or less.

The same only different
A millipede feeds mainly on plants, dead or alive. It sometimes eats dead insects or small worms. A centipede feeds on other animals, killing them with a pair of poisonous claws under the head, near the mouth. Most centipedes eat only insects but the larger ones may eat toads, small snakes and lizards.

Millipedes crawl slowly. They use their many legs for pushing through soil. Centipedes run fast. They need to do so because their prey is alive and might escape.

Another difference between the two animals is in the way the legs are arranged. The bodies of both are in rings. Each ring of a millipede body has two pairs of legs on it. A centipede has only one pair of legs to each ring.

Millipedes live in dark damp places, in the soil, in crevices in rocks or under loose bark on tree trunks. When

disturbed they curl up into a tight spiral. This leaves the tough upper surface exposed but protects the legs and soft underside. Some millipedes roll into a ball. They are called pill millipedes. When some tropical millipedes roll up they are as big as a golf ball.

Centipedes also live in damp places, coming out mainly at night to feed. They rest by day under stones, in the soil or under dead leaves. So, in the way they live, they are very like millipedes.

The largest millipede is the African snake millipede 28 cm (11in) long and 2 cm ($\frac{3}{4}$ in) across. The smallest is one living in Europe. It is only 3.5 mm ($\frac{1}{16}$ in) long. Most centipedes are about 3–4 cm ($1\frac{1}{8}$–$1\frac{1}{2}$in) long, but the giant centipede living in the jungles of Brazil is 26.5 cm ($10\frac{1}{2}$in) long.

A brightly-coloured warning
Most millipedes have stink glands along the sides of the body. Some contain cyanide. The large ones can squirt this over a distance of 5 cm (2 in) for protection. Although millipedes are mainly brown or black many of them are brightly-coloured or have patterns of coloured spots. One African millipede is bright red except for its legs and head, which are black. These colours warn other animals to keep away and so they protect the millipedes. One kind of millipede gives out light at night like a glowworm. This may be another kind of warning.

Millipedes sometimes appear in millions on main roads, on railway tracks, across farms, even in houses. When they swarm over railroads the wheels of the trains slip and traffic comes to a halt. When they swarm over farms anyone working in the fields becomes sick from the smell of them. They do great damage to potatoes and root crops.

Excellent mothers
Female millipedes make good mothers. Each lays 200–300 eggs in the soil, often in a nest. The nest is dome-shaped and made of mud, with a hole at the top. It looks like a tiny volcano. The mother

◀Some millipedes just hatching from their eggs. They will live in the damp soil of woods.

▶Centipedes are carnivorous and the one in the middle picture has just caught an insect, killing it with poison from the claws by its mouth. Millipedes, which cannot move as fast as centipedes, can climb rocks (**top**) or burrow through loose earth (**bottom**).

coils her body round the nest to protect it. From time to time she cleans the eggs.

When first hatched the baby millipedes have only three pairs of legs. They take two years or more to become full grown.

Female centipedes are also good mothers. They protect their eggs, cleaning them from time to time. They also protect the newly-hatched baby centipedes, and they lick them to keep them clean.

Many female centipedes build little mud turrets, like those the millipedes build. The female lays her eggs in the turret and then coils her body around it. She stays with the eggs until they hatch. She also stays with her young ones to protect them until they are able to look after themselves.

◀Even though centipedes do not have 100 legs, nor millipedes 1,000, these pictures show that they certainly have a lot of legs. **Left** The common millipede is dark and hides from its enemies. In contrast the centipede (**far left**) can run fast to catch the insects and small animals on which it feeds.

SCORPIONS

▲A close view of the sting in a scorpion's tail.

Scorpions are related to spiders and, like spiders, have eight legs. The 600 different kinds of scorpion live in hot countries, especially in deserts. The largest are 18 cms (7 in) long and are dark brown or black. The smallest is only 1 cm (⅜ in) long and a very pale brown or yellowish.

Large or small, every scorpion is made in the same way. The oval, flattish body is made up of a very small head, a thorax and an abdomen. On the head are a pair of pincers, like those of a lobster. The legs grow from the thorax. The end of the abdomen forms a long thin tail. At the tip of the tail is the scorpion's poisonous sting.

A dangerous tail

The pincers and the sting make a scorpion look dangerous. When disturbed it holds out its pincers and opens them wide. At the same time it curves its tail over its back, ready to stab with its sting. There are many stories about the scorpion's dangerous sting. In fact only a few scorpions have a sting strong enough to harm us. The sting from a small scorpion causes a swelling and makes the part stung go numb. This goes in about two hours. The sting from a large scorpion affects the whole nervous system and, if not treated quickly by a doctor, can cause death. The sting is used mostly in defence. Some scorpions even give a warning that they are going to attack. They rub their pincers across the front legs. This makes a noise like a

grasshopper or a cricket. Others make a noise by rubbing the legs against the pincers.

Scorpions hide by day under stones, in crevices in rocks, under dead leaves or loose bark or in the sand. Often they come into houses and hide under carpets or under beds. They may even crawl into shoes or clothes left on the floor.

Scorpions feed mainly on spiders and insects, killing them with their pincers. The stings are only used on those that struggle.

Scorpions have their own enemies. Baboons turn over stones to look for them. They know how to break off the tail and the pincers so that they do no harm. Some lizards and snakes eat scorpions. Army ants can kill them and so can some birds.

A strange dance

Scorpions have a strange courtship dance. The male grasps the female's pincers with his own. Then he walks sideways, first in one direction, then in the other. Or he may walk backwards and forwards, forcing the female to move in time with him. It looks almost like two people doing a ballroom dance. Like the female spider, a female scorpion may eat her partner after he has mated with her.

Scorpions do not lay eggs. The babies are born usually one or two at a time. Several weeks may pass before all are born. As soon as one is born it climbs onto the mother's back and she carries her babies around in this way until they are strong enough to find their own food.

There are many strange stories about scorpions. One of them is that a scorpion, if cornered or surrounded by a ring of fire, will sting itself to death rather than be captured or burned. This is probably because the heat makes the tail curve over and touch the back, so it seems to be stinging itself.

▼This drawing shows the inside of a scorpion's body.

▶This type of scorpion is extremely poisonous and dangerous even to man. It is widely distributed in Algeria, Morocco and the western Sahara.

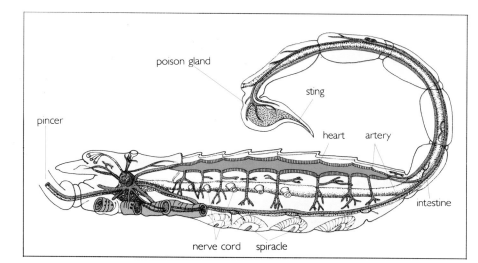

poison gland

sting

pincer

heart   artery

intestine

nerve cord   spiracle

▼The courtship dance of a pair of scorpions. The male grasps the female's claws in his own and walks backwards and forwards dragging her with him.

▼When a scorpion is disturbed it gets ready to attack. It spreads its pincers wide and brings its tail over its back. There is a poison in the tip of its tail.

GLOSSARY

Abdomen The part of the body in which the stomach and intestines are found. In insects it is the last of the three parts of the body.

Antenna (plural **antennae**) Sometimes called a feeler; the two antennae on the head of an insect are used mainly for smelling and touching.

Arthropod Short for Arthropoda, meaning 'jointed legs', the scientific name for insects, spiders, crustaceans, millipedes and centipedes.

Bristletail A tiny wingless insect with, usually three, bristly tails.

Bug A name sometimes used for all insects, but really for insects with usually flattish bodies, sucking mouth-parts and wings that are half-stiff, half-flimsy.

Chrysalis The **pupa** of a butterfly. The word comes from the Greek word for gold because a chrysalis is often a shining golden colour.

Crustaceans Animals such as crabs and lobsters with a hard, crust-like shell (*see* Arthropod).

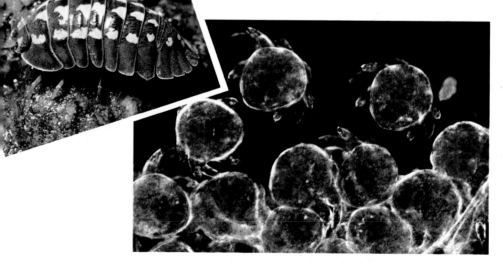

▼This woodlouse is a crustacean, but one that does not live in water.

◀ The larvae of tiny water crustaceans. When they are adults they will look like shrimps.

Decapods Crustaceans such as crabs and lobsters with five pairs of legs (**deka** is the Greek word for ten, **pous** is Greek for foot).

Flagellate A microscopic animal that swims by lashing whip-like hairs on its single-celled body (*flagellare* means to whip in Latin).

Formic acid A fluid ants squirt at their enemies. It is a weak acid that irritates the skin (*formica* is the Latin word for ant).

Fossil The remains of animals and plants that lived in past ages found in rocks or dug out of the ground.

Ganglion (plural **ganglia**) A tight cluster of nerve cells.

Grub The larva of an insect, especially one found digging or grubbing in the earth or in rotten wood.

Halteres The hind wings of two-winged flies that are now little stalked knobs used as balancers.

Honeydew Sweet, sticky liquid given out by aphids.

Invertebrate An animal without a backbone.

Labium The under-lip of an arthropod.

Labrum The upper-lip covering the mouth of an arthropod.

Larva (plural **larvae**) An insect from the time it leaves the egg until it becomes a pupa. (If the insect does not change into a pupa it is called a nymph before it is adult).

Luminous Something that gives off light.

Maggot A worm-like insect larva with no legs.

Mammal An animal which is fed on its mother's milk while it is a baby.

Mandible Each half of an insect's jaw (both halves of the beak of a bird; lower jaw of a mammal).

Maxilla (plural **maxillae**) Each half of the second pair of jaws that many insects have.

Metamorphosis A complete change in shape, as when a caterpillar changes to a pupa.

Nectar A sweet fluid found in flowers.

Pigment Colouring matter or dye.

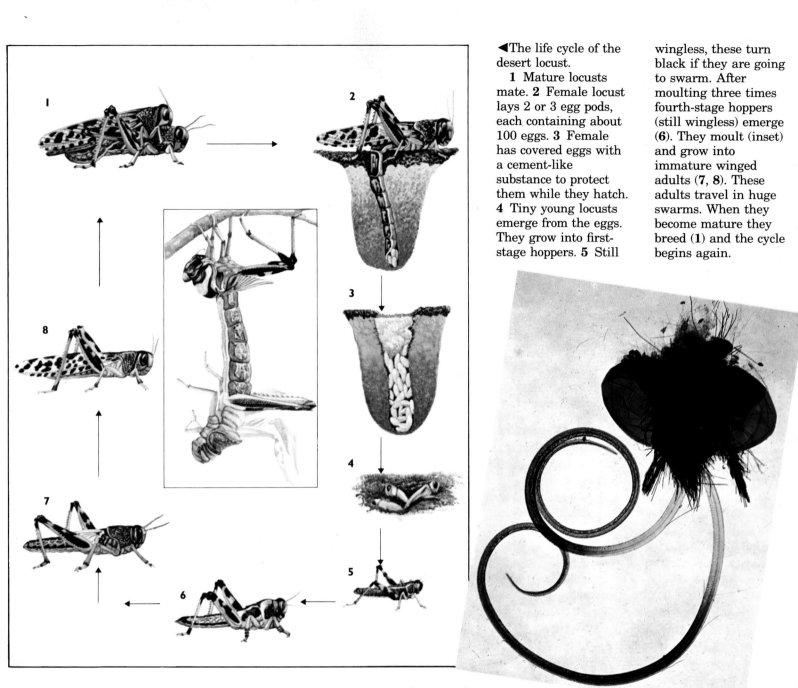

◀The life cycle of the desert locust.

1 Mature locusts mate. **2** Female locust lays 2 or 3 egg pods, each containing about 100 eggs. **3** Female has covered eggs with a cement-like substance to protect them while they hatch. **4** Tiny young locusts emerge from the eggs. They grow into first-stage hoppers. **5** Still wingless, these turn black if they are going to swarm. After moulting three times fourth-stage hoppers (still wingless) emerge (**6**). They moult (inset) and grow into immature winged adults (**7, 8**). These adults travel in huge swarms. When they become mature they breed (**1**) and the cycle begins again.

▲Part of the head of a butterfly. The two long curling projections join to form the proboscis, a tube for sucking nectar from flowers.

Palps Tiny jointed feelers, like very small antennae, on the mouth-parts of arthropods.

Pollen Tiny grains from the stamens of flowers that fertilise the seeds.

Proboscis First used for an elephant's trunk, now used for a nose or for the tubular mouth-parts of insects that feed by sucking.

Proleg One of the unjointed legs at the hind end of an insect larva, especially on a caterpillar.

Prosoma The front part of the body of a spider or a crustacean.

Pupa (plural **pupae**) The third stage in the life of many insects that comes between the larva and the adult.

Scale insect Insects related to aphids that look like green scales on the plants whose sap they suck.

Species A group of animals or plants that look alike and behave in the same way, and are different from any others.

Spinneret One of a group of tiny spinning organs on the bodies of some insects, such as silkworms and on all spiders.

Spiracle A small hole which lets air into the body of an insect.

Springtail An insect that jumps using a kind of spring under its tail.

Thorax The middle of the three parts of an insect's body.

Trace element Chemicals found in plants and animals in such small amounts that scientists knew nothing about them until early this century. They are probably important in an animal's diet.

INDEX

Acknowledgements

Heather Angel, Barnaby's Picture Library, Ron Boardman, NA Callow, Bruce Coleman, Colorific!, Archivo IGDA, J Grant, Jacana, Popperfoto, Spectrum Colour Library.